IMAGES
of America

ILLINOIS
OIL AND GAS

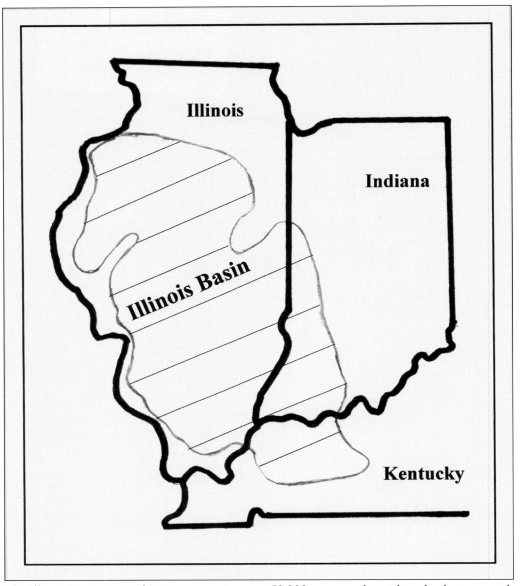

The Illinois Basin is a geologic area covering over 50,000 square miles with rocks that are a rich source of coal, petroleum, and other minerals. The basin covers a large part of southern Illinois, western Kentucky, and southwestern Indiana. The basin has produced approximately 4.2 billion barrels of oil. Oil is produced in 40 of the 102 Illinois counties. (Author map.)

ON THE COVER: This pre-1910 view from the Illinois Oil Field shows workers sitting on one of several wooden storage tanks, commonly used in the very early days of the field's development. There are hundreds of oil fields in Illinois, but in the early days of discoveries in Clark and Crawford Counties, the productive area was simply known as the Illinois Oil Field. (Author's collection.)

IMAGES
of America

ILLINOIS
OIL AND GAS

Jeff A. Spencer

ARCADIA
PUBLISHING

Published by Arcadia Publishing
Charleston, South Carolina

Printed in the United States of America

Library of Congress Control Number: 2022950061

For all general information, please contact Arcadia Publishing:
Telephone 843-853-2070
Fax 843-853-0044
E-mail sales@arcadiapublishing.com
For customer service and orders:
Toll-Free 1-888-313-2665

Visit us on the Internet at www.arcadiapublishing.com

To Illinois oil explorers, oil field workers, and oil producers, past and present.

CONTENTS

ACKNOWLEDGMENTS

In my travels through southeastern Illinois, I had the pleasure of spending an afternoon with members of the Lawrence County Historical Society. I thank Donna Burton for coordinating the meeting and arranging for me to have access to some of the society's archives; several of their images are presented in this book. Society member John King also helped decipher some names on the reverse of one of the photographs. Others who graciously provided scans of historical images were Bill Molony; David Cantrell of the Hamilton County Historical Society; Harper Saglier, Lewis University, Romeoville, Illinois; and Nick Nielsen, author of an excellent website of vintage oil and gas road maps. Martha Menser of the Oilfield Store provided a recent photograph of that historic building. Emily Spencer and Nick Rebman took several photographs of Chicago's Aon building for me to choose from. Rondel Boyd and other members of the Oblong Facebook page provided information on the murals of Oblong. Technical information on various topics and sites was provided by the Chicago History Museum and good friends Steve McDaniel and Allen Fornea. Thanks to my Arcadia editor Caroline (Anderson) Vickerson. Love to my wife, Linda, who helped with proofreading.

All images used in this book come from the author's collection unless otherwise noted.

INTRODUCTION

As early as 1865, there were attempts to drill for oil in Illinois. Arguably the first commercial oil production in the state was near Litchfield in 1882, followed by minor oil production near Sparta in 1887 and Pittsfield in 1890. A small gas well in Clark County near the town of Casey in 1904 could probably be considered the impetus for the discovery of the Eastern Illinois Oil Field the following year. The year 1905 saw many significant events for the state. Oil discoveries in western Clark County near Casey, Westfield, and Oilfield led to the first oil transported by tank cars in the state; oil production that year was over 180,000 barrels from 189 producing wells.

The Eastern Illinois Oil Field included Clark, Crawford, Lawrence, Edgar, Coles, Cumberland, Jasper, and Wabash Counties; a portion of southwest Indiana; and a small area in Kentucky. Three main areas or districts of oil production were the Northern or Shallow District, the Central or Crawford District, and the Southern or Lawrence or Deep District. The commercial centers for these three districts were Casey, Robinson, and Bridgeport, respectively. The Northern District, with initial significant oil development taking place from 1905 to 1910, produced predominantly from shallow depths of 350–600 feet until deeper production was established at approximately 2,750 feet near Westfield. The Shire oil pool discovered in 1906 near the towns of Oblong and Stoy set off the oil boom of the Central District, with the primary oil objective, the Robinson sands, drilled at depths of approximately 900 feet. That same year, town lot drilling in Bridgeport led to the Southern District oil boom.

The Western Illinois Oil Field included Marion, Clinton, Bond, Montgomery, Macoupin, Morgan, Pike, Madison, St. Clair, Randolph, Jackson, and Perry Counties. The first commercial oil production in this area was in Marion County in 1908, near a Centralia coal mine. A strong oil producer was also completed that year near Sparta in Randolph County. More significant oil production was established the following year near Centralia and Sandoval. This area saw four oil wells completed in 1909, and by the end of 1910, thirty-five wells were producing a total of 3,000 barrels of oil per day and 22 wells were drilling. Additional oil discoveries were made near Carlinville (1909) in Macoupin County and near Carlyle (1910) in Clinton County.

The rapid expansion of drilling and completion of wells in the state in these early years resulted in an increase of oil production from 180,000 barrels in 1905 to 4.4 million barrels in 1906, and from 189 producing wells in 1905 to over 3,000 in 1906. The following year, the well count had more than doubled, and total oil production reached 16.4 million barrels. The peak production over the first nine years was in 1908, with 34 million barrels of oil produced from over 11,000 wells. Oil prices from 1905 to 1911 stayed fairly stable, ranging from 59¢ to 81¢ per barrel. The Ohio Oil Company, later Marathon, quickly became the early dominant oil company in Illinois, buying up leases for oil production and pipelines. With the purchase and expansion of the Robinson oil refinery, the company also became a major oil refiner in the state.

This first Illinois oil boom brought employment and growth to the area towns. In addition to a drilling crew of four or five men per 12-hour shift, land brokers and lawyers were needed to secure drilling leases, along with workers to transport drilling materials to and from drill sites, and construction crews to assemble and disassemble the oil derricks. Nitroglycerine factories opened, and oil well shooters stimulated the wells for production. Success brought the need for oil pumpers to watch over and produce the wells and teamsters to transport the oil to central locations. As the boom continued, the railroad expanded to both serve the additional passengers and to transport pipe and other drilling equipment into the area. Soon, tank cars were transporting oil to the many small refineries opening around the state. Pipelines and pumping stations transported the oil to larger refining centers throughout the state, such as those in the St. Louis area and others in nearby states.

Larger oil companies such as Standard Oil of Indiana, Pure Oil, and Socony-Vacuum (later Mobil Oil) had major offices in Chicago. With sponsorship from the petroleum industry, the Chicago Museum of Science and Industry developed several energy exhibits over the years. The petroleum industry also exhibited at the 1933–1934 Century of Progress International Exposition along the Chicago lakefront. One notable exhibit was Sinclair Refining Company's large dinosaur models.

The state enjoyed a second oil boom, centered in Marion County, from 1937 into the war years of the early 1940s. The Centralia and Sandoval areas had experienced success in 1908 and 1909, but nothing like what the county would experience with the discovery of the Centralia oil field in 1937 and the Lake Centralia–Salem—later referred to as just Salem—oil field a year later. Less than a year after the Texas Oil Company's No. 1 Tate well discovered the Salem oil field, there were 599 producing wells in the field. Between July 1938 and July 1939, the field produced a staggering 20,080,000 barrels of oil. Largely due to Marion County, the state of Illinois produced over 470 million barrels of oil from 1941 to 1945. Pres. Franklin D. Roosevelt is said to have stated, "Thank God for Salem, Illinois." Illinois also supported the war effort as the first stage terminus for the "Big Inch," a 24-inch oil pipeline quickly constructed to transport oil from East Texas to Norris City, Illinois, where it was loaded onto railroad tank cars and shipped east.

Illinois continues to contribute to the American petroleum industry, ranking fourth in crude oil refining and 16th in oil production.

One

CLARK COUNTY

5927 Shooting an Oil Well at Westfield, Ill.

In February 1906, A.W. Lewis of the Illinois Geological Survey visited the "new" Westfield oil district to witness the rapidly developing oil field, which at the time was thought to include parts of five counties: Coles, Cumberland, Clark, Crawford, and Jasper. Wells were being drilled and completed at shallow depths from 200 to 900 feet.

The price for the shallow oil produced in the Westfield district in early 1906 was 81¢ a barrel. Standard Oil Company was the primary purchaser. The oil was said to be of similar grade to that of the Ohio-Indiana oil field. The early Westfield wells pumped at an average rate of 20 barrels per day.

Oilfield, previously known as Oil Fields and Oil City, is a former village located between Casey and Westfield. At one time, the town included a school, stores, and a hotel. The current Oilfield Store was built in 1866 as a one-room school. It later served as a general store, and is now a café renowned for its homemade pies and live music. (Courtesy of Martha Menser.)

The Ohio Oil Company, initially incorporated in Ohio in 1887, paid the State of Illinois $50 on March 20, 1905, for a license to do business in Illinois. The company opened its principal Illinois office in the town of Casey and soon opened additional offices in the Illinois towns of Robinson, Marshall, and Bridgeport. The Clark County offices in Casey and Marshall were initially in residential-looking buildings. In 1913, the Marshall office housed the company's engineering, surveying, discharge (oil pumping), and telegraph departments. The image below of the company's office in Casey presumably includes nine members of the office staff.

Railroad Depot, Casey, Ill.—49015-R

The Casey oil field opened in early 1905, and oil shipments by rail began that June. That same month, oil loading racks along the Cincinnati, Hamilton & Dayton Railway (CH&D) were constructed near the town of Oilfield. One of three railroads to operate near Casey, the CH&D had depots in Westfield and Casey. By the summer of 1906, it was not unusual to see over 50 oil tank cars pass through the Casey train depot daily, transporting oil from the nearby oil fields. The trains also provided transportation of oil field supplies to the area. Passengers arrived to see the new oil field, some to look for employment.

Casey, Illinois.   JAN 17 1907

This portable drilling rig is hidden by the flow of oil in a Clark County gusher near Casey. Compared to the drilling equipment, the gusher's height is easily 50 feet. The famous 1901 Lucas oil well at Spindletop, Texas, had an estimated gusher height of 100–150 feet.

The Leader Oil Company's Casey refinery opened for business in 1907. The Leader Pipe Line Company had gathering lines throughout Clark County transporting oil to the company's refinery west of Casey. Surplus oil was shipped in tank cars by rail to refineries in Pennsylvania. In early 1913, the company expanded its railroad lines with short spurs into the supply yards, as it was shipping 8–12 tank cars of refined oil and gasoline daily. In September of that year, the refinery experienced a disastrous fire that destroyed much of the facility.

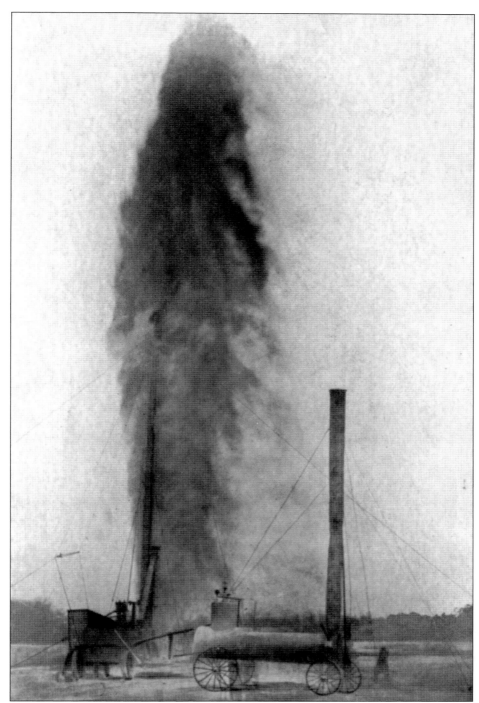

What appears to be a Star drilling machine, a common portable drilling rig in the early Illinois oil fields, is partially obscured by the flow of oil. In the right foreground is a portable boiler, known as a locomotive boiler because of its similarity to a train locomotive. The boiler provided power for the drilling machine.

Charles Johnson and Doit Young, two of several founders of Casey's Merchants and Traders Bank, formed the Casey National Bank, which was chartered in January 1906. In 1940, the Casey National Bank bought the assets and business of the First National Bank in Casey. This May 1906–postmarked First National Bank envelope includes scenes of the oil boom, which brought money and development to the Casey area.

The Cornplanter Refining Company was formed in 1888 in Warren, Pennsylvania, and operated a refinery there. In July 1907, with total capital of $450,000, the company was authorized to operate in Illinois with capital there of $12,000. By 1912, along with Sun Oil and the Missouri-Illinois Railroad, Cornplanter became a major rail transporter of oil in Crawford, Lawrence, and Clark Counties. Records suggest that Cornplanter had a strong business relationship with the Leader refinery in Casey.

By 1913, there were 14 Ohio Oil Company pumping stations in five Illinois counties, including one in Martinsville. The Martinsville oil pumping station was the main junction or "head station" in the early Ohio Oil Company system, which is evident by the large complex of buildings seen here. Constructed in 1906 and expanded the following year, the company's first major pipeline in Illinois ran from Martinsville to Preble, Indiana.

This is some of the work done out here. It is rather lonesome out here. Tell the people I am coming home after the 10th of January.

Smile

MARTINSVILLE. TANK. FARM
PHOTO BY COOLEY.

One of the earlier Illinois oil storage tank farms was in Casey, approximately a half mile north of town. The nearby Martinsville tank farm started with nine tanks, and soon the company was building four new tanks a week. At least 30 oil tanks are visible in the view below. By 1907, the Ohio Oil Company had 130 full storage tanks of crude oil in its Martinsville and Bridgeport tank farms. By 1913, the company had 235 oil storage tanks in Clark County.

BIRDS EYE VIEW OHIO OIL CO. TANK FARM LOOKING WEST
MARTINSVILLE ILL

Twenty-two men and one well-dressed woman pause for a photo opportunity during the construction of a large oil storage tank near Casey. Coincidentally, the image below of a roofing crew on a 35,000-barrel tank near Martinsville also shows 22 workers posing. Oil tank building crews were kept busy with the need for oil storage near the Clark County oil fields.

The Burning Oil Tank near Martinsville Ill.

Captions on different versions of this postcard attribute the oil storage tank fire to 13 different towns in three different states: Ohio, Indiana, and Illinois. Research strongly suggests that this scene "near Martinsville, Ill" originated from a photograph by Pennsylvania oilfield executive S.R. Ball and may have been taken in the Oil City, Pennsylvania, area around 1900.

A 35,000 Barrel Tank of Oil Burning. – Ohio Oil Co. Casey. Ill.–4800=

Newspaper articles suggest that this may be an Ohio Oil Company storage tank between the towns of Casey and Martinsville that was struck by lightning in July 1909. Oil field tank fires were common in the early petroleum years, and many were ignited by lightning strikes.

Above, over 40 employees of the Ohio Oil Company pose for a photograph in front of a burning oil tank near Casey. Some of the clothing suggests these were not workers attempting to quell the fire. Often, oil tank fires were too far advanced and were left to burn themselves out at quite a financial cost to the owners. Oil companies, including the Ohio Oil Company, would stencil large numbers on the many tanks in their oil tank farms. The burning tank at right bears the number 279.

In early July 1909, the Ohio Oil Company used a cannon to shoot holes into one of the company's 35,000-barrel oil tank near Martinsville. Much of the oil drained out of the tank and into an area enclosed by an earthen dike, but the financial loss to the company was still over $25,000.

7042 Public Highway in the Illinois Field.

Presumably a tongue-in-cheek postcard caption, this "public highway" in the early Illinois oil field was probably representative of many oil field roads. Imagine oxen or horse-pulled supply wagons dragging oil field supplies and drilling derrick parts down these types of roads in all types of weather.

Two

CRAWFORD COUNTY

In 2001, volunteers erected a 52-foot replica of the DeWitte T. Finley No. 1 John Shire wooden oil derrick. Drilled in early 1906 to a depth of approximately 1,000 feet, the well was shot and came in producing 2,500 barrels of oil per day. Treat, Crawford, and Treat leased an adjoining 80-acre tract from Dr. E.L. Birch, drilled, and brought in an oil gusher. These wells started the Crawford County oil boom. (Author photograph.)

Oil Derricks.
Oblong, Ill.
5345

An oil field scene near the town of Oblong shows a Star drilling machine to the left of two wooden oil derricks. The Star Drilling Machine Company was formed in Akron, Ohio, in the 1890s, and its portable drilling machines quickly became a favorite in the country's oil fields. The company ceased operations in the late 1940s. Different types of portable drilling rigs were used in the early Crawford County oil fields. The Parkersburg Rig and Reel Company of West Virginia was organized in 1896. By 1904, the company was producing a popular portable drilling rig that was used throughout the Midwest.

7505   A Star and a Parkersburg Drilling
Machine in Operation, Crawford Co., Ill.

24

Miller Well, Robinson, Ill.

At least three oil wells were completed on a Mrs. Miller's farm near Stoy. In June 1906, the No. 3 well came in at an estimated rate of 1,000 barrels a day. If the well pictured is indeed one of her wells, this would be one of the earliest oil gushers in Crawford County. There was also a Laughner and Miller Oil Company active in the area in 1906.

The "Pride of Crawford County" is an oil gusher on the Clark farm, northeast of Oblong. A June 1906 newspaper article reported that derricks were being "erected as fast as they can be hauled to the field." The population of Robinson had "trebled," and some people were sleeping in tents due to lack of accommodations.

Artist Robert Treece painted this mural on the side of Oblong's Harmon's Drug Store (established in 1946). The center circle, painted in 2019, shows a farming scene and an oil pump jack. In 2021, the mural was completed with the addition of an oil derrick, a Jensen oil pump jack, a train locomotive, a service station, and a bright red Ohio Oil Company truck with its marathon runner logo. (Author photograph.)

In 1989, the nonprofit Illinois Oil Foundation was formed with the mission of operating Oblong's Illinois Oil Field Museum, including a library and archives, as a source of history and education and to preserve, collect, study, and exhibit materials relating to the oil boom. (Author photograph.)

The village of Stoy in Crawford County is between the cities of Oblong and Robinson. The discovery well for Crawford County, the Shire well, was less than two miles south of Stoy. This was one of the early oil field towns and is known for a November 1911 robbery of the Stoy State Bank, where nitroglycerine was used to blow open the vault.

The Ohio Oil Company's Stoy pumping station in Crawford County pumped oil 25 miles north to the Martinsville, Clark County station, which was a main junction site for Ohio Oil Company pipelines. Before the pipeline system was completed, as many as three Illinois Central oil trains a day ran through the Stoy railroad station.

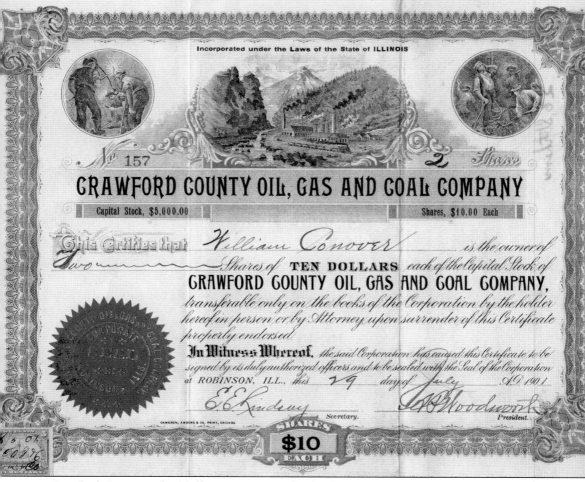

Incorporated under the Laws of the State of ILLINOIS

N° 157   2 Shares

CRAWFORD COUNTY OIL, GAS AND COAL COMPANY

Capital Stock, $5,000.00   Shares, $10.00 Each

This Certifies that *William Conover* is the owner of *Two* Shares of **TEN DOLLARS** each of the Capital Stock of **CRAWFORD COUNTY OIL, GAS AND COAL COMPANY,** transferable only on the books of the Corporation by the holder hereof in person or by Attorney upon surrender of this Certificate properly endorsed.

In Witness Whereof, the said Corporation has caused this Certificate to be signed by its duly authorized officers and to be sealed with the Seal of the Corporation at ROBINSON, ILL., this 29 day of July A.D. 1901.

E.E. Lindsay
Secretary.

A.P. Woodworth
President.

CAMERON, AMBERG & CO. PRINT, CHICAGO.

SHARES $10 EACH

Crawford County judge William C. Jones and other local businessmen organized the Crawford County Oil, Gas and Coal Company in 1901 with capital stock of $5,000. The company drilled a well to a depth of 1,010 feet on the D.C. Jones farm in 1901, encountering a small amount of gas. They drilled additional wells over the next few years but did not establish economic oil or gas production. The company issued some of the earliest stock in the Illinois Basin. This stock certificate from June 1901 was signed by A.P. Woodworth, who later owned the Woodworth Hotel.

Oblong's Colonial Hotel first opened in 1908 as the Gem Hotel. The Oil Belt Bank held meetings here, as did other oil investors. During the early boom days of Crawford County, this hotel provided some of the best accommodations in the area. It burned down in 1918.

This street view of the west side of Robinson's town square around 1909 shows the Farmers and Producers Bank at far left next to the National Supply Company. To the right of the clothing store is the Oil Well Supply Company. National Supply (founded in Ohio in 1870) and Oil Well Supply (founded in Pennsylvania in 1878) were competing companies providing oil well supplies.

The website for the Illinois Oil Museum in Oblong states that "a favorite recreation of people in 1906 was to come to Oblong on the morning train, rent a rig at moderate cost, get a map of the oil field from the *Oblong Oracle* newspaper office and drive through the countryside viewing the wells, then leave on the evening train."

A flow of oil gushing over a derrick was not an uncommon sight in the early oil fields of Crawford County. The goal was to stimulate the oil reservoir rock with an explosion of nitroglycerine, avoid any fire risk, and, after the well blew in, control the flow of oil and begin producing.

Postmarked August 1909, this postcard of a nitroglycerin explosion near Robinson, Illinois, was most likely the April 16, 1909, explosion at the Independent Torpedo Company's plant. In 1909, the company entered the Illinois oil field supply market in Robinson. It built a nitroglycerin factory about two and a half miles east of town and a magazine approximately four miles west of town. The company initially employed a state superintendent, six well shooters, and a mixer.

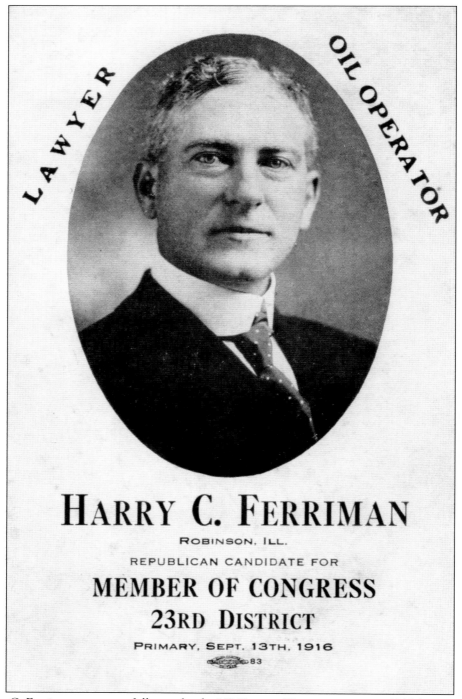

LAWYER

OIL OPERATOR

HARRY C. FERRIMAN

ROBINSON, ILL.

REPUBLICAN CANDIDATE FOR

MEMBER OF CONGRESS
23RD DISTRICT

PRIMARY, SEPT. 13TH, 1916

83

Harry C. Ferriman unsuccessfully ran for the US House of Representatives in 1916, losing to the Democratic incumbent Martin D. Foster. Ferriman, born in Olney, settled in Robinson in 1913, where he practiced law and invested in oil properties in Crawford County, becoming a successful independent oil operator and producer.

Abner Palmer "A.P." Woodworth (1829–1911) opened the Hotel Woodworth for business in Robinson in 1907. The hotel was expanded a short time later. Woodworth was an early investor in the oil business of the area, serving as president of the Crawford County Oil, Gas, and Coal Company in 1901 and 1902. The hotel at the corner of Main and Jefferson Streets was known for its many amenities, including a barbershop, billiard room, and parlor. In 1909, the Quaker City Oil Company had an office in the hotel. The hotel was razed in 1979 after a disastrous fire.

Martin No. 1, being shot, Robinson, Ills. 1,000 fee

The Red Bank Oil Company drilled at least six wells on a Martin lease in Crawford County sometime before 1913. The No. 1 well tested gas with rates as high as 1.5 million cubic feet per day. The other five wells tested oil from the Robinson sand at depths of approximately 900 feet. Two of the oil wells reported tests of 35 and 50 barrels of oil per day.

Penn Gas and Oil Company of Robinson was incorporated in 1910 and capitalized with $50,000 by W.H. Dye, F.R. Warner, and A.S. Seidel. Perhaps the W.H Dye mentioned in the captions of these two images is the same as the Penn Gas and Oil cofounder and possibly one of the men in the Buskirk derrick view at right or the man blowing off the gas of a No. 4 well below.

KEELEY OIL WELL, NEAR ROBINSON, ILL.

The Ohio Oil Company drilled at least nine Keeley wells in the Robinson area before 1913. These wells were drilled to a total depth of approximately 1,100 feet targeting what was known as the Robinson sands. Four of the wells were completed with an initial production of 10–30 barrels per day, but one tested at 100 barrels per day and another at 200 barrels per day.

Oil Well at Stoy, Ill.

A pumper going to one of his wells.

In the early 1900s, pumpers played a critical role in maintaining production from exiting oil wells, using a variety of steam, oil, and natural gas-powered internal combustion engines and pumps. Among other duties, pumpers maintained subsurface pumps that were installed inside well casings as well as pumps that were used to pump oil from surface storage tanks, earthen pits, or oil pipelines to local refineries or larger central tank farms. The five oil field workers seen below near Robinson have their occupations identified on the reverse of the photograph: "Here is the way we look in Ill. Two pumpers, two 'roustys' (roustabouts), and a teamster."

A Tank Farm and Reservoir of the Standard Oil Co. Crawford Co. Ill

Before the construction of large oil storage tank farms, large open earthen tanks or reservoirs were used as settling tanks for the produced water, sand, and silt, and for oil storage. These were commonly used throughout the oil regions of the United States, and some were quite large. Near Humble, Texas, the Guffey Company maintained a 40-acre operation of earthen storage tanks, some of which were covered with wooden "roofs." The large storage tanks were more efficient and easier to maintain, but oil companies could not build them fast enough in the early boom days.

35,000 Bbl. Oil Storage Tanks, Robinson, Ill.

Flat Car
Excursion on the Oil Belt Rail Road
July 24th 1910.
Photo by Merrick

The Oil Belt Traction Company was organized in May 1909. The Oil Belt Railway ran approximately 25 miles between the towns of Oblong and Bridgeport with the goal to both improve transportation in the oil fields and provide farmers a way to better get their products to market. Construction began on the line in 1909, but the railway did not begin operation until 1913. The short-lived venture ended in 1916.

The "Big 4" was the nickname for the Midwest's Cleveland, Cincinnati, Chicago & St. Louis Railroad, which operated from 1889 to 1930. The railroad was acquired by the New York Central in 1906 but retained as a separate entity until 1930. The railroad carried many passengers and oil field equipment during the oil boom days. The Robinson depot seen here is now the VFW Post 4549 Veterans Memorial Military Museum.

7037 Pulling Rods in the Illinois Oil Field.

Pulling and replacing worn rods and downhole pumping equipment is a common and necessary oil field practice. A rod, or sucker rod, is a solid steel or hardwood rod, typically 25 feet in length, with metal threads at both ends, connected with a metal coupling. The rod string connects the pumping apparatus at the surface with the downhole positive displacement piston pump installed inside the depths of an oil well. The basic sucker rod pumping system is one of the oldest, and still most widely used, types of artificial lift systems. In the early oil fields, power to pull the rods was provided by horses, oxen, or mules.

40

Captioned "tanks and a pool of oil, Robinson," this image shows reflections of smaller wooden oil storage tanks probably near a gathering area for a group of wells on an operator's lease, rather than a storage tank farm. Some of these types of tanks held oil, while others held produced water.

How We Make Our Money, Robinson, Ill.

Making money was certainly the goal of the early oil industry of Illinois, and the oil field workers put in long days during all types of weather. What looks like a ramshackle roof covering these drillers was all too typical of the often quickly built drill site for some of the early wells.

Storms during the summer of 1907 were devastating for oil storage in Crawford County. At least three separate storms were accompanied by lightning strikes that ignited the large 35,000-barrel tanks. During one storm, five of these large oil storage tanks were struck by lightning near Oblong.

George Rhees of Columbus, Ohio, along with T.C. Griffin and George Stephens of Findlay, Ohio, formed a corporation in July 1906 to build a refinery near Robinson to construct and maintain pipe lines and to operate for oil in the nearby oil fields. The Robinson Oil Refining Company (RORCO) maintained a blacksmith and repair shop, a dynamo house, and a barrel house not far from a railroad siding. Over 15 RORCO oil tanks cars are visible on the railroad tracks below. The refinery grew to a 750 barrel per day capacity.

The Ohio Oil Company was founded in 1887, and its initial headquarters were in Lima, Ohio. With its exploration and production start in the prolific oil region of northwestern Ohio, the company experienced strong growth. Two years later, John D. Rockefeller's Standard Oil Trust purchased the Ohio Oil Company. In 1905, Standard moved the offices 35 miles northeast to Findlay, Ohio. The Ohio Oil Company resumed independent operation in 1911 following the dissolution of the Standard Oil monopoly. Organized with a capital of $1 million, Thomas Flinn purchased the Wabash Refining Company in 1921, reorganizing as the Lincoln Oil Refining Company. In June 1924, the Ohio Oil Company purchased most of the stock of the Lincoln Refining Company, which included the 1906 Lincoln Robinson refinery. Major renovations and additions occurred at the refinery in 1927 and 1949.

The Yates Oil Field of Pecos County, Texas, is one of the largest oil fields in the United States, producing approximately a half billion barrels of oil. The field was discovered in 1926 by a partnership of Transcontinental Oil Company and Mid Kansas Oil Company, a subsidiary of the Ohio Oil Company. In 1930, Ohio Oil purchased Transcontinental, which since 1920 marketed gasoline under the name Marathon, represented by the Greek runner Pheidippides trademark and its "Best in the Long Run" slogan. The deal included wells, three refineries, and 376 filling stations. The Marathon brand proved so popular that by World War II the name had largely replaced the LINCO name at service stations. In 1962, Mid Kansas Oil Company and Ohio Oil Company became Marathon Oil, officially changing its corporate name in conjunction with its 75 anniversary.

In 1924, the Ohio Oil Company purchased the Lincoln Oil Refining Company, consisting of the Robinson, Illinois, oil refinery and 17 LINCO service stations in Illinois and Indiana. After the purchase, the company expanded into the upper Midwest and retained LINCO as the main brand until the late 1930s. (Courtesy of Nick Nielsen.)

Three

LAWRENCE COUNTY

High-rate gas wells, or "gassers," in the Bridgeport area could often be heard roaring for miles. Estimated rates of five million cubic feet of gas per day were not unusual around 1909. A spark could set a gas well aflame, but sometimes the gas was purposefully lit to show off potential to investors or impress crowds. Night views of burning gas wells were especially impressive.

Burning Gas well. Bridgeport, Ill. 10890

In 1906, some of the earliest productive wells in Lawrence County were drilled on town lots in Bridgeport. There were no spacing or safety requirements in these early days of Illinois drilling. If there was a space on a lot large enough for a derrick and the mineral interest leased, a well could be drilled. Even with the wells being drilled in such close proximity to each other, there were many very profitable town lot wells.

Among the Derricks in West Bridgeport, Ill.

In the summer of 1907, the town of Bridgeport took possession of a Revolutionary War–type cannon and three boxes of four-inch iron balls. The cannon was 10 feet long with a four-inch bore and mounted on wheels. It was purchased for shooting holes into the large oil storage tanks when they caught fire, letting the oil out of the tanks and into the area surrounded by earthen dikes.

The Lawrence County oil field was discovered in 1906. By 1912, seven productive sands had been discovered from approximately 700 to 2,000 feet deep. Local names, such as Bridgeport, Buchanan, Kirkwood, Tracey, and McClosky, were assigned to the oil zones. The McClosky lime was especially prolific in the area.

Edward A.L. Roberts patented the Roberts Torpedo in 1865 as "an exploding torpedo to fracture oil-bearing formations to increase oil production." Initially, the explosive material used in the torpedo was gunpowder, but by 1868, nitroglycerin was generally preferred.

Dozens of onlookers examine the crater caused by an explosion of nitroglycerine. Charles Townsend, an oil well shooter from Lawrenceville, was hauling the explosive from a Stoy factory to the storage magazine on the Lee Dunlap farm near Bridgeport. The explosion occurred as Townsend was crossing a concrete bridge, where apparently a jolt caused the nitroglycerine to explode. The driver was killed, the truck was blown to bits, and storefronts in Bridgeport were damaged. (Courtesy of Lawrence County Illinois Historical Society.)

Shooting an oil well Lawrenceville, Ill.

"Shooting" a well is a method of stimulation to increase the flow of oil. In the early days of oil well completion, this was often accomplished by lowering a shell or torpedo filled with gunpowder or nitroglycerine into a wellbore and then detonating the explosive material using a variety of methods. Transporting and working with nitroglycerine were dangerous professions.

BRIDGEPORT, ILLINOIS

These views of early drilling derricks show some of the key parts of the system. To the left above is a locomotive-type boiler, common among the early standard oil boilers. It resembled the boiler of an early train engine. Some models were portable, with large wheels for movement between drill sites. The layout would consist of a locomotive boiler, then the steam engine in a roofed space, followed by the beltway to the walking beam unit in the standard derrick. This was considered the safest arrangement and was common from the mid-1870s into the 1900s.

"Oil Derrick," Bridgeport, Ill.

Divers Farm, Bridgeport, Ill.

Oil was discovered in 1906 by the Jennings Producing Company on John Divers's 35-acre farm one mile south of Bridgeport. Within a short time, there were 15 producing wells on the farm, and in three years, the cumulative production was approximately 1.4 million barrels of oil. When Divers died in 1918, his obituary said that he was "one of the most prominent and influential citizens of Bridgeport." In June 1909, lighting struck a 35,000-barrel Ohio Oil Company oil storage tank on the Divers farm. Holes were shot into the tank, and part of the oil was saved. Two years earlier, another destructive oil fire had occurred on this same farm.

BURNING OF OIL TANKS DIVER FARM BRIDGEPORT. ILL.

Teams of oxen often handled the transportation of the heavy oil field equipment. Teamsters preferred oxen over horses and mules to maneuver through muddy roads. A yoke of oxen is a team of two; the wooden beam between the pair is also called a yoke. The top of an oil derrick peeks over the building in the above view. One 1908 newspaper article stated that "a peculiar result of the oil boom" was that the "patient and steady-going ox" had "again come into its own." An expert ox driver with a three-yoke team could command $16 a day working in the oil field. The Ohio Oil Company's supply yard near Bridgeport contained large amounts of well casing and other pipe as well as boilers.

Bridgeport's business section grew with the Lawrence County oil boom. The Big 4 Oil and Gas Company was one of the larger oil companies in the area by the mid-1920s. In 1926, the company operated 105 wells and employed 25 workers. Next door to the Big 4 office is the Oil Well Supply Company. With its origins in the Pennsylvania oil fields of the 1870s, this company had offices throughout the oil towns of the United States. Oil storage tanks were often in close proximity to a railroad line. Below, Big 4's 37,500-barrel tank sits by a loading rack and side track near Bridgeport around 1907. There were oil loading racks near Bridgeport and Lawrenceville linked to the Baltimore & Ohio Railroad. An oil derrick is barely visible at far right.

One of the 37,500 Barrel Oil Tanks and Loading Rack With Oil Cars on Side Track, Bridgeport, Ill.

Oil storage tank designs varied, but a common early size was 30 feet high and 90 feet wide. They were made of 5- by 10-foot riveted iron plates that tapered from a half inch on the bottom ring to a quarter inch on the top two rings. They had a roof of riveted iron plates and were supported by eight-by-eight-foot timbers. Each tank held 35,000 barrels of oil, weighed over 1.2 million pounds, and was surrounded by a four-foot fire wall. (Above, courtesy of Lawrence County Illinois Historical Society.)

Thunderstorms during the summer of 1909 were especially destructive to the oil fields of Lawrence County. Several oil storage tanks were struck by lightning and burned. One tank was reported to have burned for four days. These images of Ohio Oil Company storage tank No. 241 burning on June 28 illustrate just some of the damage caused by lightning strikes that year.

35,000 Barrel Steel Tank of Oil, Struck by Lightning June 28, 1909, Bridgeport, Ill.

STRUCK BY LIGHTNING JUNE 28 09 BRIDGEPORT ILL

The Ohio Oil Company operated a series of pumping stations to transport oil through a pipeline system. The Bridgeport pumping station in Lawrence County had a 1914 capacity of 60,000 barrels of oil, which could be pumped with a pressure of 800 pounds to the next station 25 miles to the northwest in Stoy. Early smaller pumping stations might be set up for a small field or collection of wells and often had smaller wooden tanks in several sizes for storing oil or produced water.

Employees of the Ohio Oil Company's Bridgeport Production Company District 9 pose for a photograph in front of the T.I. Gould tool house in 1947. From left to right are (first row) Leonard Gray, Dale Weaver, J.O. Beard, Clifford Holmes, Frances Wagner, Ralph Hudson, Paul Dean, E.B. Peters, James Puntney, Bryl Satterthwaite, Gene Carl, Everett Smith, George Goodhart, and Leslie Jones; (second row) Leland Gray, Elmer Meeks, Joe Anderson, Ervin Forsythe, Leroy Foster, Willard Morehead, Ernie Dunham, George Bell, Isom Dunham, and Howard Green; (third row) Gerald Biethel, unidentified, Tom Mills, John Odonley, Ernest Roan, Gene McAdow, Sylvan Hutchings, Fred Goodhart, Frances Weaver, Noble Spond, Arthur Turner, and Paul McGuire. (Courtesy of Lawrence County Illinois Historical Society.)

Lawrenceville's Indian Refinery opened in 1907. The company purchased the Havemeyer Oil Company and the Havoline name in 1909 and immediately began producing and marketing Havoline products. The company expanded again in 1920 with the purchase of the stock of the Central Refining Company, which operated a refinery just north of the Indian Refinery. The Indian Refining Company's corporate office moved to Lawrenceville from New York three years later. (Both, courtesy of Lawrence County Illinois Historical Society.)

State Bank, Bridgeport, Ill.

With the strength of the local oil industry, Bridgeport banks remained solvent and strong during the financial crisis of 1907. Four banks were operating in Bridgeport at the time: Bridgeport First National Bank, Farmer's Bank, Bridgeport Banking Company, and the Bridgeport State Bank.

OIL FIELDS, SUMNER, ILL. 36

Instead of powering each well pump jack, a more economical and efficient system of pumping dozens of low-rate oil wells was used in many very shallow oil fields, such as this example near Sumner. Using a central power plant, often with a natural gas engine, a system of shackle lines radiated out from the power plant pumping the oil wells.

.BRIDGEPORT OIL FIELDS.

Postcards were very popular with vacationers in the early 1900s. This unusual aluminum or tin postcard depicts a Bridgeport oil gusher. Though commonly composed of various types of cardboard, postcards were occasionally made of wood, metal, or cork. Transferring the image onto the material was a difficult process. Often, mailing these postcards without an envelope was prohibited by postal authorities.

A lightning strike in October 1909 ignited two 37,000-barrel oil storage tanks near Bridgeport, causing a loss of over $150,000. Cannons were dispatched to the fires, but with no effect. Several smaller wooden oil tanks were also destroyed. The storm season of 1910 began with a lightning strike near Bridgeport, which ignited another oil storage tank. Here, over 70 men with shovels pose after working to stop an oil tank fire from spreading.

In 1906, the Ohio Oil Company leased 826 acres from Perry King. By late 1913, the company had over 25 oil wells on the lease. The Ohio District 10 Perry King toolhouse was presumably on the King lease. Robert Spaulding, foreman, is perhaps the central figure in this 1938 company photograph of 47 workers. (Courtesy of Lawrence County Illinois Historical Society.)

With the early town lot drilling in Bridgeport, it appears that the Ohio Oil Company's pipe yard was not far from the action. Drilling pipe and casing of all sizes are stacked in what appears to be a residential area of Bridgeport, with a side railway used to transport pipe.

In 1932, the Ohio Oil Company began construction on a company machine shop east of Bridgeport on the Joe Griggs farm. The size of the initial building was 30 feet by 80 feet. Being the dominant major oil company in the early Illinois oil fields, the company had facilities across the major producing areas of the state.

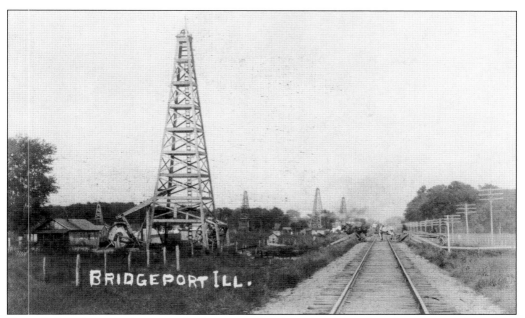

Five oil derricks very close to a Bridgeport railroad track suggest that this is a spur line for a main railway line, constructed close to an oil field to better facilitate the moving of the oil to a main line.

Five people, including two girls in dresses, pose in front of a small pumping facility near Bridgeport. The tilted stack is probably from the boiler that powers a pumping unit. Smaller wooden oil storage tanks store the oil.

The Indian Refining Company of Lawrenceville greatly expanded during the 1920s and became a major refiner and shipper of oil products. The company developed its Waxfree Havoline Motor Oil using a solvent dewaxing process. This process and product attracted the Texas Company (later Texaco), which acquired majority control of the Indian Refining Company on January 14, 1931. The acquisition included the Lawrenceville refinery, the process, and the Havoline trademark. The company expanded the refinery in 1933, and in 1934, Texaco began marketing its Havoline Waxfree Motor Oil. The Lawrenceville refinery was closed in 1985. (Below, courtesy of Lawrence County Illinois Historical Society.)

Four

RICHLAND, CLAY, AND WABASH COUNTIES

Pure Oil Company made a major discovery in Richland County's Clay City oil field in May 1937 with the drilling of the Bunny Travis well. Early tests of the well saw rates of over 2,500 barrels per day. By late 1937, there were 11 producing oil wells on the Travis farm. An exuberant farmer and lessor, Travis purchased every workman on the well a new suit.

Richland and Clay Counties experienced an oil boom beginning in 1937. Steel derricks were everywhere. Between May and August, the population of Olney increased from 6,100 to 8,000 and the population of Clay City from 600 to 1,800. Due to a housing shortage, the boomtown of Bunnyville was built on the Bunny Travis lease in October. The town included 13 cottages, a boardinghouse, a bunkhouse, an office, and a warehouse.

This Pure Oil Company camp, captioned "N.W. of Fairfield, Ill." (Wayne County), is probably the company's camp to the north near Clay City (Clay County), constructed in the late 1930s. Clay County is north of and adjacent to Wayne County. Pure Oil was a major player in Richland and Clay Counties.

With its success in the Olney area, Pure Oil Company built a new office in the town in 1937. On March 10, 1961, the company donated this and other buildings to the East Richland Unit District 1. A year later, the office building was renovated and became the foundation for the newly established Olney Community College.

Noble, Illinois. Largest Oil Field in the Southern Illinois Basin. Driving through Noble on U. S. Route 50 there are Oil Wells as far as the eye can reach in every direction.

The Ohio Oil Company discovered oil a mile northwest of the town of Noble in Richland County in July 1937. Later that year, the residents of Noble placed a banner over Route 50 declaring, "Noble, The Oil Center of the World." The Pure Oil Company was another large player in the development of the oil field, which progressed into the Shafer addition on the north side of town.

McCawley Baird Well
North Olney Field
Olney, Illinois

After drilling several dry holes north of Olney in the spring and early summer of 1938, the Texas Company drilled and completed the No. 1 McCawley Baird well, initially flowing 260 barrels per day from the McCloskey zone. This extension to the north of the previous Olney drilling became the North Olney oil field. The spring of 1938 saw some impressive well tests. The Pyramid Oil Company completed its No. 1 University of Chicago well for 1,010 barrels per day.

Oil production was established north of Flora in Clay County in 1938. In addition to smaller operators, Carter Oil Company was an active driller in the area. Its Neely (Neeley) well, two miles north of Flora, drilled and completed in July 1938, initially tested 150 barrels per day from the McCloskey lime. The average cost to drill a 3,000-foot well in early 1938 was approximately $25,000.

First Oil Well in Wabash County, Allendale Ill.

Wabash County's Allendale oil pool was discovered in 1912. The field was in the eastern portion of the county, approximately 20 miles south of Lawrenceville, and in 1913 was considered a southern extension of the Lawrence County oil district. A significant extension to the field occurred in 1922 initiated by the completion of an especially good well on the Delta Wright farm.

Five

WHITE COUNTY

STORMS DISCOVERY WELL, CARMI, ILL

In June 1939, the Angle and Eason No. 1 Storms well blew in at an estimated rate of 8–15 million cubic feet of gas per day, approximately six miles south of Carmi in White County. The drilling crew was able to cap the gas well after it ran wild for several days. By the end of the year, approximately 20 companies were active in the area and 13 wells had been successfully completed.

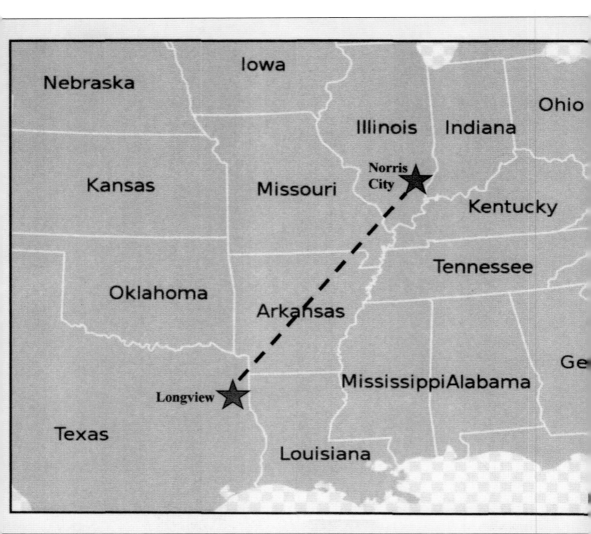

The War Emergency Pipeline, nicknamed the "Big Inch," ran from Longview, Texas, 531 miles to Norris City, Illinois. Work began on this first leg of the pipeline on August 3, 1942. The laying of pipe began near Little Rock, Arkansas, followed by other crews starting segments elsewhere in Arkansas and Texas.

A four-foot deep, three-foot wide ditch was dug for the 24-inch diameter steel pipeline. Crews could lay as much as nine miles of pipeline a day. The pipeline passed under 33 rivers, over 200 creeks and lakes, near approximately 300 railroads, and over 600 highways. (Courtesy of Library of Congress.)

Railcars transported hundreds of loads of pipe to the Big Inch construction areas. Each segment was up to 44 feet in length and weighed on average 4,200 pounds. Most oil pipelines were no greater than eight inches in diameter, making the Big Inch quite an engineering feat. (Courtesy of Library of Congress.)

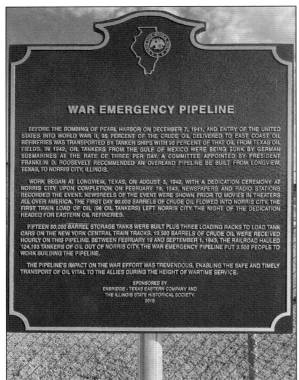

The first phase of the pipeline ended at Norris City, 12 miles southwest of Carmi. Here, oil from the pipeline was loaded onto railroad tank cars. The oil would then move by rail to the East Coast. Later, the second phase of the pipeline was completed from Norris City to Phoenixville, Pennsylvania. The first oil arrived at Norris City on February 19, 1943. (Author photograph.)

Booster stations along the line pumped the oil at a rate of four miles per hour. The completed Longview to Phoenixville pipeline was 1,254 miles long with 28 pumping stations approximately 50 miles apart. Longview was pumping station No. 1; Norris City's pumping station was No. 11. (Courtesy of David Cantrell, Hamilton County Historical Society.)

In 1942, Williams Brother Corporation of Tulsa, Oklahoma, became an important figure in the oil and gas pipeline construction industry, as it was designated the principal contractor for the Big Inch project. Fifteen crews of 300–400 men drove trucks, handled earthmoving equipment, and laid and welded pipe. One method of welding was stovepiping, where the pipe remained stationary and the welder worked his way around the pipe. Once the Big Inch was completed to Norris City, a second leg was constructed from Norris City to Phoenixville, Pennsylvania. The first crude oil arrived at Phoenixville via the Big Inch on August 14, 1943. The Big Inch was sold in 1947 and converted to a natural gas pipeline. (Both, courtesy of Library of Congress.)

Established in 1950, Central Supply Company has served the Illinois Oil Basin for over 71 years. Located in the town of Crossville, seven miles north of the White County seat of Carmi, the innovative company sign includes tools of the oil field: bails, swivel, hook, and fish tail bits. (Author photograph.)

Six

WESTERN COUNTIES

In April 1911, a new oil field was discovered three miles northwest of the Clinton County town of Carlyle. Within five months, 24 oil wells had been completed in the area. Some sources rated the field as the best new field of the year east of the Mississippi. The Ohio Oil Company bought out many leases from small independent oil companies in the area.

BEN SCHOMAKER No I. BHS
SURPASS WELL SHOT JUNE 28 '11.
CARLYLE — ILL.

OIL WELL, CARLYLE, ILL.

By the end of 1912, the Surpass Oil and Gas Company of Pittsburgh, Pennsylvania, was one of the largest oil producers in Clinton County. When the company, with W.W. Laird as president, sold its Carlyle assets to the Ohio Oil Company in January 1913 for approximately $250,000, Surpass was producing 800 barrels of oil per day total from 57 wells and held 800 acres.

In the late 1800s to early 1900s, as US travel greatly increased, there was a demand for souvenirs. Images, many taken from postcards, could be printed onto pieces of china, including plates, cups, bowls, vases, mugs, sugar bowls, creamers, candlesticks, pitchers, bells, toothpick holders, and steins. Oil field scenes were among the images used on souvenir china pieces, including this view of an oil well near Carlyle.

F.B.RANGER No 10
SMITH FARM
CARLYLE — ILL.
BMS

Frank B. Ranger, formerly from the southeast Ohio oil center of Marietta, had early 1911 drilling success on the Smith farm near Carlyle. In December 1911, he sold his 900 acres and 16 wells with total daily production of 600 barrels to the Ohio Oil Company for approximately $200,000. Ranger then retired to California.

A well drilled on the Hubert Schlafly farm near Carlyle in May 1911 encountered high grade, dark, "sweet" (non-sulphur) oil in the 820-foot sand. When the well came in, estimates placed the rate at 500 barrels per day. Another well in the area on the McCabe farm tested approximately two million cubic feet of gas per day from the same 820-foot sand.

Attempts to discover oil near Hoffman in Clinton County began as early as 1908. With the great success in Marion County's Centralia field in 1937 just east of Hoffman, renewed activity led to the discovery of the Hoffman oil field in 1939. By 1944, there were 44 oil wells in the field.

Scene in Oil Field. Taggart Well in Foreground Sparta, Ill. 2713

In early 1908, two Taggert wells on the McIlroy farm near Sparta caught the attention of Standard Oil. Rumors were that the company had purchased large holdings of real estate in and around Randolph County. After two years of marginal production in the area, the Taggert No. 1 well tested at over 100 barrels of oil per day. A local laundry business included a gushing oil well on its advertising postcard.

COMPLIMENTS OF   SPARTA OIL WELL.

THE HOME LAUNDRY,
H. H. WILLIAMS, PROPRIETOR.

EVERYTHING BACK BUT THE DIRT,
SATISFACTION GUARANTEED.

OFFICE AND PLANT
ON SOUTH ST. LOUIS STREET.   SPARTA, ILL.

Shooting for Oil, Birmingham, Ill.

The town of Birmingham is in Schuyler County. By 1913, only four wells had been drilled near Birmingham, all by the Schuyler Oil and Gas Company. Though unsuccessful, the information gained from drilling these wells led to the discovery of the Colmar field, approximately seven miles northwest in McDonough County.

Several unsuccessful attempts were made to establish oil production around 1910 near Pickneyville in Perry County, southeast of St. Louis. Additional attempts just south of Pickneyville in Jackson County had similar results. The reverse of this postcard included the comment, "Afraid it isn't much of an oil well."

"Oil Well" Pinckneyville Illinois

Prospectors leased approximately 30,000 acres near Carlinville in Macoupin County. In 1909, a gas well was completed on the Klein farm, testing approximately three million cubic feet of gas per day. As commonly done, the gas was ignited at night and burned to a height of 25 feet to demonstrate the well's potential to a large group of spectators.

DRILLING FOR OIL ON KLEIN FARM.
CARLINVILLE ILL. APRIL - 1909.

DRILLING GAS WELL SOUTH OF CARLINVILLE, ILL.

The Carlinville area was known for its coal production, which began in 1867. Standard Oil purchased leases and a coal mine in the area in 1917, as coal was used in the refining of crude oil, and Carlinville was situated between the company's Wood River, Illinois, and Whiting, Indiana, refineries. The oil and gas produced from the Carlinville field is associated with coal seams and interbedded sandstones.

HENRY KOLMER OIL WELL NO. 3

The first big oil well in the Waterloo-Columbia oil field of Morgan County was the No. 1 Robert Frierdich. This well produced from an oil sand at approximately 400 feet, as did the offset No. 2 well. Three Henry Kolmer wells were completed near the Frierdich wells. The Kolmer No. 1 well tested at approximately 175 barrels of oil per day.

In September 1908, hopes ran high for the Sparta area and newspapers were making comparisons to not only the Casey area in Clark County but also to Beaumont, Texas (Spindletop). Pennsylvanian J.D. Hoblitzelle, who had also had success near Casey, had completed his fourth well, testing over 130 barrels per day.

Standard Oil Company's Wood River/Alton refinery in Madison County was built in 1907. The first oil on the 126-mile journey from Martinsville arrived on Sunday, December 22 of the same year. Initially, the refinery's main products were heating oil, paraffin, kerosene, and asphalt. With the rapid growth of the automobile industry, the refinery later produced motor oils. Before the Ohio Oil Company established its refining business in Illinois, the company sent much of its oil

to Standard's refinery. In 1926, Standard Oil spent $100,000 to build a swimming pool, at the time the largest in the country, for the Wood River community. In 1956, Standard Oil of Indiana became Amoco and kept the refinery going until its closure in 1981. The company closed the Wood River chemical additives plant in the 1990s. (Above, courtesy of Library of Congress.)

SHOOTING AN OIL WELL, EDWARDSVILLE

2B27

In 1907, several companies attempted to discover oil in Madison County, near the town of Edwardsville. After almost a year of drilling, success was finally achieved by two companies, the Charleston Crude Oil Company and the Charleston Pipe Line Company, drilling approximately six miles south of town.

Seven

MARION COUNTY

The Burton Brothers, with offices in Sandoval, rigged up a derrick on John Shanklin's farm in July 1909. Brother Nelse Burton claimed that he had 25 years of experience as a driller. The well reached a total depth of 1,559 feet and was completed in October. By April of the following year, the company had this well and a second well on the farm producing approximately 300 barrels of oil per day.

SHOOTING BURTON BROS. OIL WELL SHANKLIN FARM, SANDOVAL, ILL, OCT. 2, '09.

SHOOTING FIRST OIL WELL AT
CENTRALIA, ILL. NOV. 1-'08.
MADE FOR CENTRALIA BOOK STORE

Operators were aware of an oil seep associated with a fault in the coal mine between the towns of Sandoval and Centralia in Marion County. In 1908, the Marion Oil and Gas Company drilled a well a half mile east of the mine on the Sherman farm but only encountered slight shows of oil. Three additional wells were drilled southwest of the Sherman well that year, with initial rates of 18 barrels per day, but the rates quickly dropped to three barrels per day. Additional drilling occurred in early 1909, leading to more significant oil tests.

SHOOTING SECOND OIL WELL,
CENTRALIA, ILL. JAN-22-'09

In the spring of 1909, the No. 1 Stein well tested 50 barrels of oil per day from a depth of 1,404 feet. The productive sand was then named "Stein sand." This well is often considered the discovery well for the Sandoval oil field. While the Stein well was being drilled, another well, Champaign's Southwestern Oil and Gas Company No. 1 Benoit, was drilling just 1,200 feet to the southeast. The Benoit well drilled deeper than the Stein well and encountered oil at a depth of 1,540 feet. This productive oil sand was designated the "Benoit sand." These two wells helped set off a drilling boom in the area. By April 1910, Southwestern had six wells producing in the field for a combined rate of approximately 1,000 barrels a day.

STEIN GAS AND OIL WELL, SANDOVAL, ILL. FIRST PRODUCER IN THE FIELD.

SHOOTING BENOIST OIL AND GAS WELL, SOUTHWESTERN OIL AND GAS CO. SANDOVAL, ILL. JULY 14, 1909.

In this "View from Ohio Oil Co. Tank Warfield No. 1 Sandoral Oil Field. Odin, Ill.," at least eight wooden oil derricks are easily visible. Sandoval is misspelled "Sandoral," and Odin is four miles east of it. A Southwestern No. 1 Warfield well was drilled in the same section, 5-2N-1E, as the Stein discovery well. Perhaps this well was purchased by the Ohio Oil Company, or there was an Ohio Oil Company well later drilled on a Warfield lease.

With the rapid development of the Sandoval oil field, employment greatly increased. Preparing oil well drill sites, transporting equipment, drilling and completing the wells, and getting the oil to market all required a large workforce. More than 20 workmen pose for a photograph during the building of an Ohio Oil Company 40,000-barrel oil storage tank at Sandoval.

SHOOTING FOX OIL WELL NO. 2 JULY 14, 1909.
NORTHWEST OF ODIN. ILL.

The Fox No. 2 well was drilled 1,000 feet east of the Stein well. It was thought to be farther from the oil field's edge, as its rates of 300 barrels of oil per day were stronger than the rate of the Stein well. A July 22, 1909, newspaper headline read, "Odin is Oil Wild." During that summer, several oil companies opened offices in Odin.

The Adams Oil and Gas Company drilled and completed the No. 1 Louis Schmitz as Marion County's Centralia oil field discovery well. Completed in late November 1937, the well tested 156 barrels per day. The seismically defined prospect was drilled approximately two miles northwest of Centralia.

A month after the Schmitz discovery, Shell Petroleum drilled and completed its No. 1 Earl Criley, offset to the Schmitz well, as the confirmation well for the Centralia oil field. Continued drilling concentrated on the west side of the city and then within the city limits. Townsite drilling proved a challenge to develop well-spacing restrictions.

Lake Centralia Field
Centralia Illinois

Within three months of the Centralia discovery well, leasing was at a frenzied pace for both townsite lots and farmland. Over 30 wells were drilling or preparing to drill. The hotels in the area were filled to capacity, oil field businesses were looking for office space, and housing was at a premium.

The 1938 discovery well for the Lake Centralia oil field was drilled approximately a half mile from the western shore of an artificial reservoir, Lake Centralia. Eventually, many wells were drilled along the reservoir's shoreline. As the field was developed farther to the northeast, nearing the city of Salem, the oil field's name was changed to Lake Centralia–Salem and later simply the Salem oil field.

The Texas Oil Company (later Texaco) discovered the Salem oil field in Marion County with the completion of its No. 1 E. Tate well on June 21, 1938. The well was drilled to a depth of 1,918 feet and tested 732 barrels of oil and 175,000 cubic feet of gas in a 23-hour period.

On February 1, 1939, there were 599 producing wells in the Salem oil field from three producing zones, the deeper of which, the McClosky lime, averaged 1,130 barrels per day from 64 wells. In the first year of production, from July 1938 to July 1939, the Salem oil field produced 20,080,000 barrels of oil. The January 1939 posted oil price was $1.15 per barrel. (Courtesy of Library of Congress.)

Arthur Harvey (1896–1976) first entered the oil business by purchasing a percentage of lease royalties in the East Texas oil field. With some financial success, he formed the Tex-Harvey Oil Company and ventured into the oil fields of Marion County in 1939. The company was involved in the discovery and development of the county's Tonti oil field. Harvey experienced continued success in the oilfields of West Texas.

The Centralia-Salem oil field was covered in the Jun 10, 1940, issue of *Life* magazine. A *Life* photographer flew over at night and was impressed with the flaring gas. The magazine claimed that "Centralia is the newly richest, loudest, and lustiest town." At that time, Illinois ranked third in the United States for oil production. (Courtesy of Library of Congress.)

With possible influence from the oil state of Texas, The Lone Star café offered 24-hour service in the midst of the Salem oil field. (Courtesy of Library of Congress.)

By October 1940, there were 119 producing oil wells on the J.R. Young lease near Centralia. Oil revenue help finance a church, the Young Chapel. During one week in 1940, the Salem field produced approximately 220,000 barrels of oil, and hundreds of derricks were visible in the area's fields, roads, and urban areas.

The Lake Centralia–Salem oil field in Marion County was formally unitized on September 1, 1930, for simultaneous water flooding of five pay horizons. The unitized oil field included an area of 8,800 acres approximately 6.5 miles in length and 2.5 miles in width. It was hoped that this secondary oil recovery method, water flooding, would recover a large amount of oil.

"A CHRISTMAS TREE" OIL FIELD
SALEM, ILL.

June 1943 was the fifth anniversary of the Salem oil field. The field covered approximately 10,000 acres and cumulative oil production was 172 million barrels. An oil field "Christmas tree" is an assembly of valves, spools, and fittings used for an oil, gas, or other type of well. It is named for its resemblance to a decorated tree at Christmas.

Eight

CHICAGO AREA

Originally known as the Jewelers Building, this Classical Revival–style structure at 35 East Wacker Drive on the southwest corner of North Wabash Avenue (tallest building at right center) was constructed in 1926. Pure Oil Company purchased this Chicago landmark in 1928 and occupied the building until its sale to North American Life Insurance Company in 1962. This view of the 1931 Chicago skyline includes the Carbide and Carbon Building, Mather Tower, Tribune Tower, and Wrigley Building. (Courtesy of Library of Congress.)

THE PURE OIL COMPANY, LEMONT, ILL.

In July 1954, the Pure Oil Company purchased the Globe Oil and Refining Company's Lemont oil refinery on the southwest side of Chicago. Operations at the refinery began in 1925, and Globe purchased the refinery in 1929. The multimillion-dollar transaction added 47,500 barrels of oil per day refining capacity to Pure Oil's growing market needs in the Midwest, resulting in a total refining capacity for the company of 170,000 barrels per day.

The Pure Oil Research and Development Center opened in 1950 and consisted of five redbrick buildings on 68 acres on the north side of Route 14 west of Main Street in Crystal Lake. When opened, over 200 Pure scientists, lab workers, and technicians were on the staff. In addition to administration offices, the complex included chemistry labs, a supply center, an automotive lab, a chemical engineering lab, and a boiler plant.

In 1911, the Karpen Brothers Furniture Company built its 13-story headquarters at 910 South Michigan Avenue in Chicago. The company sold the building to the Standard Oil Company of Indiana in 1927, and that same year, more stories were added to the structure. In the 1950s, a 70-foot by 76-foot Standard Oil logo was added to the roof of the building facing Lake Shore Drive. In the mid-1950s, it was claimed to be the largest neon sign in the country. Standard moved to a new building in 1974. The building had several tenants in the following years and was eventually converted into condominiums.

The 83-story Aon Center in downtown Chicago was completed in 1974 as the Standard Oil Building and nicknamed "Big Stan." With the company's name change, it became the Amoco Building in 1985. The building was originally clad in Italian Carrara marble, which suffered from permanent warping and was replaced in 1991 with North Carolina Mount Airy white granite. The building was renamed the Aon Center in 1999. (Courtesy of Emily Spencer and Nick Rebman.)

*Peoples Gas Light & Coke Co. Bldg.,
Michigan Ave. and Adams St.,
Chicago.*

Chicago's Peoples Gas Building is a 21-story office structure at 122 South Michigan Avenue. The building was constructed from 1910 to 1911. People's Gas Light & Coke Company was chartered in 1855 and provided gas to residents a few years later. After several mergers in the late 1890s, the company also sold gas stoves. In the 1920s, the company began buying natural gas from Texas instead of producing gas from coal and oil.

The Buckingham Building at 59–67 East Van Buren Street in Chicago is a 27-story structure that opened in 1930. An early tenant of the building was the Vacuum Oil Company, which merged in 1931 with Standard Oil Company of New York to become the Socony-Vacuum Company. With increased rental space acquired through the 1930s and the signing of a 10-year lease in 1940, the structure was renamed the Socony-Vacuum Building. The very visible trademark sign of the Pegasus, a winged horse, was placed on top of the building. The building was listed in the National Register of Historic Places on August 10, 2000. Buckingham Fountain, seen below, sits in the middle of Grant Park.

Gulf Exhibit at the World's Fair,
A Century of Progress, Chicago, Ill.

The Gulf Oil exhibit at the 1933–1934 world's fair in Chicago included the world's largest auto cylinder, a reproduction of the world's largest atmospheric vacuum still, and the airplane motor that set the world's endurance record. "A Century of Progress" was the slogan for the fair, which ran from June 1 to November 1, 1933, and from May 26 to October 31, 1934. Chicago's lakefront provided the scenic location; 39 million people attended the fair.

Chicago's Johnson Oil Refining Company produced advertisement ink blotters with different scenes from the 1933 Century of Progress International Exposition. Homer Johnson, previously treasurer of the Indian Oil Company, along with his brothers, formed the Johnson Refining Company in 1910. Their initial facility moved from South Chicago to Galesburg the same year and then back to Chicago Heights in 1913. The Gaseteria Company purchased Johnson Oil Company in 1956.

SINCLAIR DINOSAUR EXHIBIT AT THE CENTURY OF PROGRESS EXPOSITION

Sinclair Refining Company's world's fair exhibit included a life-sized brontosaurus (apatosaurus) as well as a stegosaurus and a *Tyrannosaurus rex* in an outdoor setting produced to resemble a dinosaur habitat of 100 million years ago. Visitors passed through a cave to learn about the origin of oil deposits. Sinclair Refining Company registered as a trademark the popular green Dino (pronounced Dye-No) dinosaur in 1932. The company's original advertising campaign included several different dinosaurs, but a single Dino emerged as the company's choice to appear on its gas station signs and on popular promotional material.

Sinclair Oil Exhibit
A Century of Progress

HAVOLINE THERMOMETER *Century of Progress International Exposition* CHICAGO 1933

Advertised as the world's tallest thermometer at 21 stories (218 feet), the Havoline Thermometer, sponsored by the Indian Refining Company of Lawrenceville, was a landmark at Chicago's 1933 Century of Progress International Exhibition. "Havoline Waxfree Motor Oil" is the advertisement at the base of the thermometer.

The first *Petroleum Age* oil industry journal was published in Bradford, Pennsylvania, from 1881 to 1888. The second journal to use the title was published in Chicago from 1914 to 1928. The publishing of the journal moved around the city, with offices on Jackson Street, Dearborn Street, East Jackson Street, and in the Great Northern Building on West Jackson Boulevard. The company also maintained an office in New York City.

Chicago's Museum of Science and Industry was founded in 1933 and occupies the Palace of Fine Arts, constructed for the 1893 World's Columbian Exposition. With an endowment from Julius Rosenwald, president of Sears, Roebuck, and Company, the museum opened in 1933 during the city's Century of Progress exposition.

One of the Museum of Science and Industry's early permanent exhibits was the Story of Oil. In 1955, the museum added to the exhibit with If Oil Vanished. In 1967, Standard Oil of Indiana provided a financial grant for "the world's most extensive petroleum exhibit" to include everything from exploration to retail supply of products. Opened in May 1968, the exhibit included an Exploration to Production Theater and a Risk Tower. The People's Gas Company sponsored a natural gas exhibit in 1975, which included a circular, nine-screen Theater of the Future presenting what life might be like in the 21st century with the possible advances in the use of natural gas. The exhibit also included the history of natural gas production in the United States and the manufacture of synthetic gas. Standard Oil Company sponsored a new petroleum exhibit in 1976 where visitors rode pods wired for sound for a 10-minute trip through 8,700 square feet with 23 sections about how oil and gas are formed and modern methods of recovery.

HOW OIL IS REFINED
AN EXHIBIT IN THE MUSEUM OF SCIENCE AND INDUSTRY, CHICAGO

NOW, YOU CAN

Check Fuel Oil Deliveries

— just as you check purchases
of gas, electricity, water, gasoline

You are invited to read the accurate meter on our truck, at start and at finish of delivery. Sealed and certified, the meter measures every drop delivered into your tank. It is positive insurance against errors . . . proves you get all you pay for.

This easy-to-read meter on our truck has a "dollar and cents" value to you.

PHONE KEDZIE 2215

PEERLESS OIL COMPANY
327 South Kedzie Avenue   CHICAGO, ILLINOIS

Peerless has been used as a company name for many years, and there have been Peerless Oil companies in Louisiana, Texas, California, and Kentucky. The Peerless Oil Company of Chicago was organized in 1914. J.E. McArdle, president, and A.L. Ardle, secretary-treasurer, are listed at the company's 1924 address of 521 West Sixty-sixth Place in Chicago. Ink blotters were popular in the days of fountain pens, with most advertisement blotters common from the 1920s to the 1950s.

The 1950 Chicago fair spanned over 60 acres of the lakefront. The Petroleum Service Center on the main plaza included facilities for rest, relaxation, information, and moving pictures. Sponsored by major oil companies and related associations, the center's movies presented the story of oil from discovery through production, transportation, refining, and marketing. No petroleum products were offered for sale in the building.

In 1981, Texaco closed its Lockport, Illinois, refinery after 70 years of operation. The refinery and oil tank farm were located along the Chicago Sanitary and Ship Canal on the north side of the city. During the war years, the refinery produced aviation gasoline, lubricating oils, and fuel oils. The refinery also produced diesel, asphalt, and coke. It achieved its maximum output of 80,000 barrels of oil per day during the 1970s. After the refinery closed, some of the coking unit was dismantled and sent to the company's Puget Sound refinery. (Above, courtesy of Bill Molony; right, courtesy of Lewis University.)

The Ohio, the American, and the Western Gas Associations merged to form the American Gas Institute, which held its first annual meeting in Chicago from October 17 to October 19, 1906. By the following year, the organization included 1,200 members who were predominantly managers of gas plants throughout the United States. In June 1918, the organization merged with the National Commercial Gas Association to form the American Gas Association, a group that is still very active today and represents more than 200 local energy companies throughout the United States. (Courtesy of Library of Congress.)

Nine

OTHER AREAS AND TOPICS

Horse-drawn Standard Oil Company wagons were common in both rural and urban areas of the United States in the late 1800s and early 1900s. Some wagons had separate compartments for different petroleum products, such as kerosene and lubricating oils. The total capacity of these tanks could be as high as 500 gallons.

MICA AXLE GREASE IS THE BEST

Trade cards, or Victorian trade cards, were a common and inexpensive form of advertisement from 1875 to the early 1900s. Petroleum-related trade cards include illuminating oil or kerosene, lubricating oils and greases, and engine oils. The Mica Axle Grease Company and the American Lubricating Company merged in 1878 and later became part of Standard Oil Company. Mica axle grease continued to be manufactured by the Standard Oil Company. With facilities in Alton and Peoria, Illinois, the Consolidated Tank Line Company became part of the Standard Oil organization in 1890 with a stock trade between the two companies. Standard Oil retained 57 percent of the company, and Consolidated served as a "jobber" for Standard. A jobber buys wholesale petroleum products and sells them to retail marketers and businesses.

In 1908, brothers Frank P. Welch and James M. Welch saw a business opportunity to market oil directly to consumers. Steady growth allowed them to incorporate the Illinois Oil Company in January 1914 as an oil refiner and distributor of petroleum products, paints, and greases. The company formed a relationship with the Illinois Refining Company and the Kawfield Oil Company, resulting in the operation of a refinery in Cushing, Oklahoma, and a barrel, paint, and grease factory in Rock Island, Illinois. By 1922, sales were $18 million, and the company's sales territory had expanded to include Minnesota, Wisconsin, Kentucky, Tennessee, Oklahoma, Arkansas, Illinois, and Iowa. These two advertisement postcards, postmarked in 1912 and 1914, provide sales information on the reverse sides.

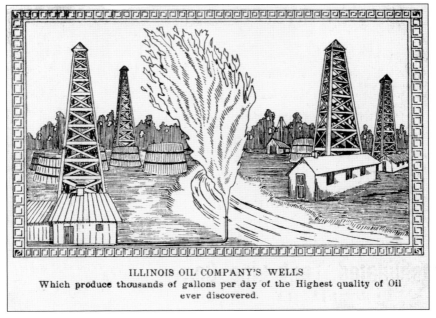

ILLINOIS OIL COMPANY'S WELLS
Which produce thousands of gallons per day of the Highest quality of Oil ever discovered.

The 1920s saw rapid growth in the use of farm tractors as more competition occurred in farm equipment manufacturing, bringing the purchase costs down. International Harvester, Case, and John Deere introduced their tractor-pulled combines. Nine local agricultural supply cooperatives formed the Illinois Farm Supply Company in 1927. Member farmers could collectively purchase petroleum products, including gasoline, kerosene, lubricating oil, and grease. Products included Penn Bond motor oil, Blue Seal motor oil, Blue Seal Wintermaster antifreeze, and Aladdin gasoline. Through a series of mergers and acquisitions, the company is now Growmark Inc.

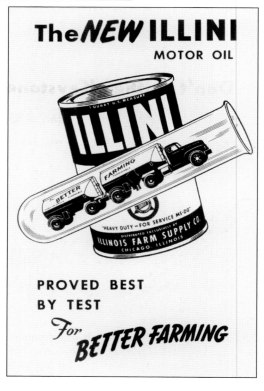

C.U. Williams of Bloomington, Illinois, aggressively marketed real-photo postcards using professional-quality photographs. The company produced several oil-related postcards between 1908 and 1915 from Illinois as well as Texas, Ohio, Oklahoma, Arkansas, Indiana, and Kansas. Realizing the growing popularity of automobiles, in 1911, Williams opened a four-story automobile showroom and garage in Bloomington. The company followed that success with the formation of the Williams Oil-O-Matic Heating Corporation, a successful manufacturer of home oil burners.

The Keystone Lubricating Company was founded in 1884 by E. Leslie Frer in Philadelphia, Pennsylvania. In the early 1900s, the company was known for Keystone Grease. The firm was purchased by Kerns United Corporation in 1962 and then by the Pennwalt Corporation in 1968. In 1988, Pennwalt was acquired by Elf Aquitaine SA, which was acquired by Total SA in 1999. In 2006, Keystone lubricants were renamed Total lubricants.

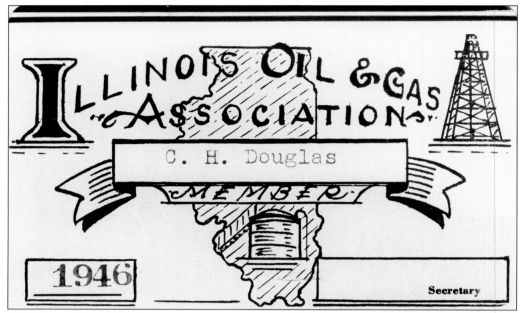

The Illinois Oil and Gas Association was organized in 1944, two years before this 1946 membership card was issued. It is dedicated to the interests of oil and gas producers and others associated with the oil and gas industry in Illinois.

The Illinois Pipe Line Company was incorporated in November 1914 in Findlay, Ohio. The company was created as a subsidiary of the Ohio Oil Company and then spun off in 1915. The company operated in the states of Illinois, Ohio, Indiana, Kentucky, Wyoming, Montana, and Texas. An early company project was the construction of a 30-mile oil pipeline from the Big Muddy oil field to refineries in Casper, Wyoming. The company again became part of the Ohio Oil Company in 1930.

Carter Oil Company maintained its Fayette County St. Elmo district office on the southeast edge of the Loudon oil field. Discovered in 1937, Loudon was the company's largest Illinois oil field during the mid-1940s. The company also provided housing for employees within three camps near the field: Fortner, with 52 houses; Williams, 4 houses; and Altamont, 28 houses.

In the early 1910s, the Prairie Oil and Gas Company operated a series of oil pumping stations from Humboldt, Kansas, to Griffith, Indiana. Located approximately 40 miles apart, one of these stations was near Wilburn, Illinois, in Marshall County and had a daily pumping capacity of 73,500 barrels of oil.

OIL WELL IN THE CHARLESTON OIL FIELD,
CHARLESTON, COLES COUNTY, ILL.

When the Eastern oil field was being developed and its boundaries tested, oil wells were completed in southeast Coles County. In 1913, two attempts were made to establish oil production near the town of Charleston; both were failures. The second well was drilled to a depth of 895 feet on the Fulton farm and abandoned after reporting no signs of oil and encountering saltwater. Later in the 1940s, oil fields such as the Mattoon were developed in the county.

The Dale Consolidated oil field of Franklin, Hamilton, and Saline Counties was discovered in 1940. Development of the field was rapid; one rural school near Hoodville announced a 30-day vacation starting in late December 1940 so a well could be drilled nearby. The field's oil and gas composition were favorable for butane production, and the Texas Company began construction on a refinery and casing-head gas plant in 1942. Butane was used to produce aviation fuel, which was in high demand for the war effort. The casing-head gas plant produced butane, isobutane, propane, isopentane, and pentane plus from 1942 to 1964. (Both, courtesy of David Cantrell, Hamilton County Historical Society.)

Oil well near Boyd, Ill.

This 1910 view of an oil derrick drilling near Boyd in Jefferson County shows a locomotive-type portable boiler in the foreground. Though difficult to see, there are a few people near the base on the derrick. Two of them are identified on the reverse of the photograph as "the girls Freda and Flossie." The Boyd oil field was not discovered until 1944. Sixteen oil wells were drilled that year and completed from approximately 2,150 feet from the Benoist and Aux Vase sandstones.

BIBLIOGRAPHY

Arnold, H.H. Jr. "Salem Oil Field, Marion County, Illinois." *AAPG Bulletin*. American Association of Petroleum Geologists, 1939.

Blatchley, Raymond S. "The Illinois Petroleum Fields." *Bulletin of the American Geographical Society*, Vol. 44, No. 6, 1912.

———. *The Oil Fields of Crawford and Lawrence Counties*. Illinois State Geological Survey, Bulletin No. 22. Urbana, IL: University of Illinois, 1913.

———. "Petroleum in Illinois in 1912 and 1913." Illinois State Geological Survey *Circular*, No. 8, 1913. Illinois State Geologial Survey, 1914.

Connelly, Dwight, and the Clark County Historical Society. *Clark County*. Charleston, SC: Arcadia Publishing, 2009.

Frankie, Wayne T., Bryan G. Huff, Russell J. Jacobson, Myrna M. Killey, David L. Reinertsen, and Vicki May. *Guide to the Geology of the Casey-Martinsville Area, Clark and Cumberland Counties, Illinois*. Champagne, IL: Department of Energy and Natural Resources, Illinois State Geological Survey, 1994.

Illinois Oil & Gas Association: Celebrating 50 Years, 1946–1996. 1996.

ioga.com

Manning, Victoria, and Jeff A. Spencer. "Greetings from Oil Country: Shared Images of a Burning Oil Tank across Five States." *Oil-Industry History*, Vol. 15. Petroleum History Institute, 2016.

mayberrytownship.net/hamilton-county/hoodville-dale-refinery

oilcompanyroadmaps.com

oldgas.com/info/texacohist

petroleumhistory.org

Spence, Hartzell. *Portrait in Oil: How Ohio Oil Company Grew to Become Marathon*. New York, NY: McGraw-Hill Company, 1962.

Spencer, Jeff A. "The Independent Torpedo Company—Oil Well Shooting in the Lima-Indiana Oil Fields and Beyond." *Oil-Industry History*, Vol. 18. Petroleum History Institute, 2017.

———. "C.U. Williams (1867–1953): Petroleum Postcards to Oil-O-Matic Burners." *Oil-Industry History*, Vol. 21. Petroleum History Institute, 2020.

theonlyoblong.com/oil_field

Wallace, Evelyn M., and Sue Jones. *Robinson and Crawford County*. Charleston, SC: Arcadia Publishing, 2006.

Wheeler, H.A. "The Illinois Oil Fields." *AIME Transactions*, Vol. 48. American Institute of Mining, Metallurgical, and Petroleum Engineers, 1915.

Discover Thousands of Local History Books
Featuring Millions of Vintage Images

Arcadia Publishing, the leading local history publisher in the United States, is committed to making history accessible and meaningful through publishing books that celebrate and preserve the heritage of America's people and places.

Find more books like this at
www.arcadiapublishing.com

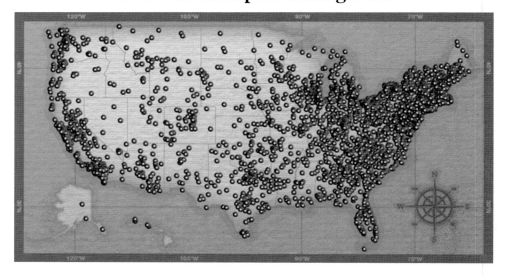

Search for your hometown history, your old stomping grounds, and even your favorite sports team.

Consistent with our mission to preserve history on a local level, this book was printed in South Carolina on American-made paper and manufactured entirely in the United States. Products carrying the accredited Forest Stewardship Council (FSC) label are printed on 100 percent FSC-certified paper.